Longer Walks on
the North York Moors

With thanks to Doug, for his
company and support.

Longer Walks on the North York Moors

by

V. Grainger

Dalesman Books
1988

The Dalesman Publishing Company Ltd.,
Clapham, via Lancaster, LA2 8EB.

First published 1988
© V. Grainger, 1988

ISBN: 0 85206 935 9

Printed by Fretwell & Cox Ltd.,
Goulbourne Street, Keighley, West Yorkshire, BD21 1PZ.

Contents

Introduction

HAVING spent many years walking on other British hills, it has been a pleasure for me to return to walk on the North York Moors, the scene of my first pleasurable introduction to the hills in the company of the Hull CHA Rambling Club. More recently, with other walking clubs and friends, I have enjoyed further exploration of this fine walking area.

Rarely in Britain do there exist areas where the National Park Authority, landowners, walkers and other countryside users co-exist in such compatibility as here, despite increasing use of and subsequent pressures on the land. In this area it is still possible for considerate walkers to have relatively unrestricted access to the countryside. With the help of footpath and bridleway signs, stiles and gates erected at the instigation of the National Park Authority, easy route finding exists throughout the Moors.

The longer walks contained in this book range from thirteen to nineteen miles in length. All of them are circular and start from reasonable car parking places. Some cannot be reached by public transport. Each route has been selected to cross as varied a range of scenery as possible in a single walk. Together they provide examples of the full range of scenery of the North York Moors.

You will walk the escarpment of the Cleveland Hills, wild heather moorland, beside sparkling becks and rivers, in woods and forests and superb dales, sheep-dotted hillsides and valleys. Throughout the year, you will be startled by the sudden explosions as the grouse leap into the air in panic. In spring, the haunting calls of the curlew are all around. But mostly you will feel the tranquility and the silence of the wild places.

In order to concentrate on the routes, details of geology, flora and fauna, historical and archaeological notes, local folklore, dialects and recipes, have been omitted from the text. A bibliography of suitable publications containing such very useful supplementary information can be found at the end of the book. When short winter days prevent long walks, further pleasurable hours of reading about the area can increase one's appreciation of the delights in store.

More and more people are taking to the hills and it is vital that we treat the land properly. Keep to the footpaths, especially across farmland, and if you open a gate, shut it again afterwards. Never climb over a dry stone wall unless it has a stone step stile in it. These walls are costly to build but easy to destroy. Follow the Country Code at all times. Avoid leaving litter and keep dogs and children under control at all times.

This beautiful countryside is our heritage but always consider the people who get their livelihood from the land. Avoid being a nuisance to others—and that includes other walkers as well as farmers and landowners.

Although the walks do not involve anything more than moorland walking, most of them are quite strenuous, and some involve two thousand feet or more of ascents overall. Unless you are very fit, the longer ones need the extended daylight hours of British Summer Time. In any case you should always allow plenty of time.

Regarding timing; in good conditions Naismith's Rule is reasonable—three miles per hour plus half an hour per thousand feet of ascent. Thus for Walk 4, allow six and a quarter hours plus stops. But don't forget that the stops include time taken to consult the guide books or maps; this alone can add on an extra hour to your estimated time.

In very wet conditions you will do well to make two and a half miles an hour so the time would be extended by another hour. If there is any chance that you will end the walk in the dark, remember to carry a good torch.

With one or two exceptions, all of these walks follow public rights-of-way. The routes have been carefully checked, and the help given by the North Yorkshire Moors National Park Office and the Forestry Commission is gratefully acknowledged. The exceptions include a short stretch on the Lyke Wake Walk and on permitted forestry paths, which are noted in the relevant text.

Together with the sketch maps provided, the routes are described in sufficient detail for the user to follow them without any other aids. However, it is always possible to take a wrong turning and it is strongly advisable—as well as more interesting—to carry the appropriate maps with you (see end of this introduction).

It is also strongly advisable to carry a compass for all of the walks. Compass directions and Grid References are given at intervals in the text. The Moors seem a very friendly place on a warm summer day but the weather can change very rapidly and for most of the year they should be treated with the utmost respect. Cold, heavy rain and mist can all appear very suddenly. Furthermore, when the heather is growing strongly, some of the footpaths are so indistinct that they can be missed altogether. A compass helps you to follow the right path, in the right direction!

The other necessities of moorland walking are, of course, essential. Good walking boots, waterproofs, extra items of warm clothing, food, a first aid kit and a survival bag for emergencies should be carried. Remember that denim jeans give no warmth when wet, so trousers or breeches should be made of other material. Don't take unnecessary risks.

****

Regarding maps, all walks are on the 1:25,000 North York Moors Outdoor Leisure Maps, East Sheet and West Sheet. These Ordnance Survey Leisure Maps are recommended but the 1:50,000 Landranger series is also useful. These, or the Ordnance Survey one inch to the mile North York Moors Tourist Map, will also allow you to locate the starting points for the walks. The latter map is also useful for locating distant scenery.

****

1. Sutton Bank–Gowerdale–Ryedale–Rievaulx

Distance: 16½ miles.
Start: Sutton Bank car park off the A170. GR 515830.
Maps: NYM Leisure Map. West Sheet.
        Landranger 100.
Conditions: Varied scenery. Fairly level and easy going.

ON leaving the car park walk towards the edge of the escarpment, then turn right on the well-defined path of the Cleveland Way.

Follow the escarpment edge in a NW direction, later veering roughly north for a distance of 2½ miles. As you proceed, look downhill and left to Gormire Lake, then pass through disused quarries and, later, beside the ruins of High Barn. Shortly afterwards, veer away from the wall on your right and descend on grassland to a gate.

Cross the minor road and enter woodland by another gate straight ahead. On passing Low Paradise Farm on the left, continue on a

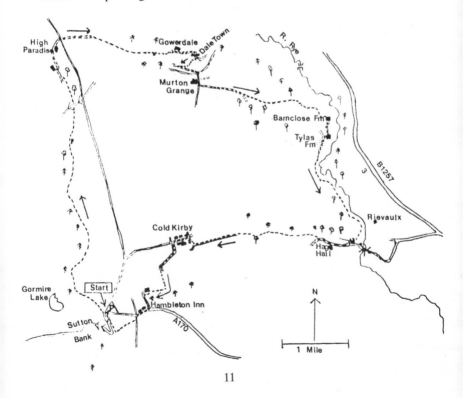

tarmac road past High Paradise Farm to a T-junction at the Hambleton road.

Go over the road and through a gate almost directly opposite to enjoy gentle walking on a grassy path going due east. Keep beside the wall and fences and continue in the same direction along the edge of several fields, enjoying improving views of the Hawnby district as you go.

Before the barn in the last field, go right through a wall and left through a gate, then straight ahead descending over rough ground. Just below a ruined building, bear right on a clear track which curves downhill then goes straight ahead through a gate in the wall.

Descend further to the valley floor of Gowerdale and pass to the right of the uninhabited house. Through a marked gate, go down the valley for 350 yards, to the corner of a fenced field on the left.

Turn right and go uphill, to join and go left on a farm track leading to the farm buildings at Dale Town. Pass through two gates between the buildings, then turn right past a large tree to climb uphill beside rough hedging and fences. When these end, go right, along an overgrown track as far as the wood, where a U-turn to the left is necessary. Now follow the clear forest track climbing more gradually uphill to a gate beside a road.

Cross straight over the road, to continue on a tarmac road to Murton Grange. Go past all the buildings, then turn left and east through the first double iron gate onto an unsurfaced road.

This road is known as Ox Pasture Lane. It passes through fields, then continues alongside woodland. At a stile follow the lane forward towards woodland on the left. Pass to the left of a barn and continue until the forest ends, then fork right going SE.

At a T-junction, turn right on a track which climbs gently. At the highest point in the field, turn left to Barnclose Farm on the signposted path which runs along the field edge, becoming a rough track through woodland. Continue on the farm track past the farm, then on a tarmac road to Tylas Farm.

Swing right between the farm buildings, and go uphill to a cross-roads. Turn briefly left on the road, and walk on beside a fence until at the lowest point of a dip in the road, leave it through a metal gate on the left, going south.

Now the route continues in pleasant riverside meadows, heading SE, with the River Rye on the left. Keep well to the right to skirt a large ox-bow, and look for glimpses of Rievaulx Abbey through the trees. The village of Rievaulx, and the abbey, built as the first Cistercian church in England in 1131, are well worth a visit.

Soon afterwards, pass through a gate into Ashberry Woods

before taking a left fork downhill to Ashberry Farm. Cross a small bridge to the main Helmsley—Scawton road. At this point your route rejoins the Cleveland Way which returns, over the next five miles, to the starting point.

Turn right and walk along the road, passing Hagg Hall, until at a point where the road bears left, turn right through a Forestry Commission gate. Continue on a well defined Forestry track through the woodland in Nettledale, passing a series of small lakes on the right. At the time of writing, these lakes housed a large and varied duck population.

At a junction of paths, go right over a wooden footbridge and through a kissing gate into deciduous woodland, joining a broad track and heading west.

Turn left at the next Y-junction, then shortly afterwards bear right on a narrow footpath which climbs gently through woods, continuing as a dry steam bed. At the top, go forward along the left edge of two fields, heading west, then between hedges on an unsurfaced road. Passing a building on the right, the road swings left, after which you turn right on a footpath through fields towards the village of Cold Kirby.

Pass the church on your left, and continue on the main road through the village. On reaching the last house on the left, turn left on a broad track to eventually cross a stile into a field. Walk down the left side, then go through a gate and head towards a woodland where another stile in a wall is crossed. Go right on the footpath beside the forest.

Where the path and forest swing left, continue forward over a stile beside a gate and straight across the field to another stile. The buildings of Hambleton House are passed to your right.

Follow the rough road left. It becomes surfaced before joining the A170 at the Hambleton Inn. Go right, crossing the busy road with care and continue, briefly, until turning left on a minor road signposted to White Horse Bank. Almost immediately, turn off to the right on the Cleveland Way.

The well-defined path passes through woodland with an earthwork known as the Eastern Dyke running beside it on the right. Soon you will reach more scenic and open views at the escarpment edge of Sutton Bank. Turn right at the edge, to enjoy the sight of Gormire Lake and the expansive Vale of York once more, as the path heads N to the car park. Cross the A170 with care and return to your starting point.

2. Kepwick–Dalicar Bridge–Thorodale Circular

Distance: 14 miles.
Start: Kepwick village. GR 467908. Limited space for car parking near the church.
Maps: NYM Leisure Map. East Sheet.
    Landranger 100.
Conditions: Mainly dry walking in woodland, valleys and meadows. Ascents about 1,600 feet.

WITH Kepwick church on your right, walk briefly forward along the tarmac road and turn left through a white gate into a field. Climb quite steeply, following a sunken track to a gate in a stone wall. Continue uphill on a clear path through bracken and occasional wild rhododendrons, keeping to the left side of the sunken track for the driest walking.

Walk beside the forest wall, and, ignoring the first gate at a corner, swing briefly left and continue uphill beside the wall, bearing left around Gallows Hill.

On passing the next gate in a broken down wall, turn immediately right through another. Go forward and turn left on a broad forest track. After a few yards bear right on a track which climbs gently through mature forest to the wide gate at Steeple Cross. The name refers to the upright stone, seen to the left on the right hand grass verge of the Hambleton Road.

Once through the gate, turn right on the old drover's road, now the route of the popular Cleveland Way footpath. Continue, firstly through forest, then past a gate, on a wide grassy avenue between stone walls.

After approximately one mile, where the Cleveland Way turns right, turn left through a gate onto a pleasant footpath along the right hand side of a field, heading east. At the end of this first field, and before the gate, turn left and head north, beside a wall. The path veers leftwards away from the wall through rough grassland. After crossing a shallow valley, bear slightly right and uphill to a gate which is about 40 yards to the right of a square, brick structure. Continue, now heading eastwards, along the left side of several fields, passing to the right of High Buildings, a group of storage barns.

Keep on through a gap in the wall on a clear cart track. When the track forks, stay on the main track to the left, which gradually descends beside woodland. When the woods end, the track leads

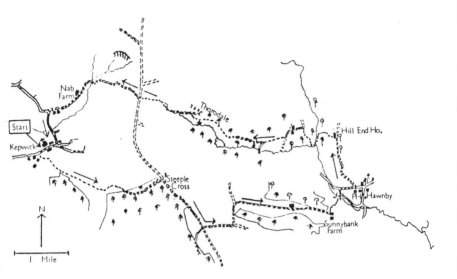

through a gate then forks in front of the buildings of Sunnybank Farm. Take the lower, left fork, then almost immediately turn left before the barn and descend to a gate, where a signpost indicates a left turn to Dalicar Bridge.

Follow this green track though another gate where you bear sharply right and descend beside a beck to a stile by a gate. Follow the beck left then drop right over rough ground, curving round a tin hut into a meadow. Walk down the left side of the meadow to a wicket gate, then cross Dalicar Bridge to join the tarmac road. Now turn left, then right at the T-junction.

For refreshments, continue for a short distance further to Hawnby and the Hawnby Inn. Otherwise at Manor Farm, turn left (NW) on a cart track. Take the higher route of 1½ miles to the uninhabited Hill End House. Turn left through a gate before the house, and descend to another gate in the bottom right corner of the field. After the next gate, turn left downhill at the field edge to yet another gate.

Continue, on a grassy path in woodland, swinging right then left and south beside the River Rye. Cross it at a metal footbridge. Go through a gate, then follow the path south to the next gate and turn right and west to another, small, footbridge. After another gate, join a clear track which heads north and leads, with occasional views to the right of the whaleback of Hawnby Hill, through woodland and fields.

On meeting a broad farm track, turn left along it to Mount

Pleasant Farm. Go between the buildings, fork left and over a cattle grid. Notice the sign warning of a bull, and hurry the few yards to cross into a field through the first gate on the right. Walk along the edge of two fields, and after a gate, go forward across an angled track and gently uphill into pleasant woodland.

Continue, ignoring all deviations, on a path which undulates gently through the woods. You may glimpse Thorodale Lake below on the left, in rare gaps between the trees.

Eventually, drop gently to a gate and enter the lovely open valley of Thorodale. Continue downhill to the beck but do not cross it. Follow the path, firstly along the valley floor over sometimes boggy ground, then rightwards uphill through bracken. A pause to look back at the view is worthwhile when some height is gained.

On meeting a wall turn right beside it, then cross a stile and walk beside another wall to a gate. Continue, keeping left of a disused quarry, to join the broad drover's road again.

Turn right on the road for a few yards and, on passing the ruins of Limekiln House on your right, where the road becomes walled on both sides, turn off left through a wooden gate. Go down hill to the right of a wall, passing an old but well-preserved kiln and a gate, then cross the beck by a small stone bridge.

Follow the path as it swings left towards Nab Farm, which is passed on the farm track to the left of the buildings, using the gates. This is confirmed as the right of way, although when you have passed the farm you will see a notice on the gate to a field on the left indicating another route. However, this is not a right of way but a concessionary path only, and subject to change.

Now continue on the farm access road to the tarmac road and turn left towards Kepwick. Go through the village to the church.

3. Fangdale Beck–Brewster Hill–Hawnby–Lower Ewe Cote Circular

Distance: 13 miles.
Starting point: Limited car parking space on the side of the road, by the footbridge and telephone box, just past the turn-off to Fangdale Beck from the main road: B1257 (GR 572948).
Maps: NYM Outdoor Leisure. West Sheet.
     Landranger 100.
Conditions: Rough moorland, tracks, and meadowland. Ascents about 1,400 feet. Compass essential.

WALK west towards the village of Fangdale Beck along the tarmac road. On reaching a road junction, take the right fork and walk through the village, with the beck on your left. At the end of the road walk on straight ahead into what seems to be a private, gravelled, driveway. Then turn right to walk between a house and a bungalow and into a short enclosed lane, through a green metal gate.

Walk briefly forward and on passing the first wall running uphill on your left, pass through a gate to walk uphill keeping the wall on your left. Continue uphill, passing through all gates. After the last wall, continue climbing on a sunken track through the bracken. Follow this diagonally rightwards up the hillside to the edge of the moor.

Follow the path which runs NW across rough moorland, passing through a gap in the last wall. The sunken path gradually peters out but the path continues, sometimes indistinctly, through heather. The path climbs gradually over occasionally wet ground, continuing in a NNW direction. Keep parallel to Fangdale Beck and aim to stay roughly between the Bilsdale transmitter on the right and the beck on the left.

The path is difficult to trace at times, but you should continue in a NW direction, skirting boggy ground on the left. Aim for the head of the valley, noting the point at which you pass the TV mast on the right and quarries on the left. At this point keep looking ahead for a path running across at right angles, faintly marked but indicated by white marker posts.

On meeting the path, follow it in a SSW direction until it becomes clearer. At this point the distinct landmark of High Thwaites, an uninhabited farmhouse in a group of deciduous trees, is seen ahead.

Head for the corner of the farm wall along the now clear farm

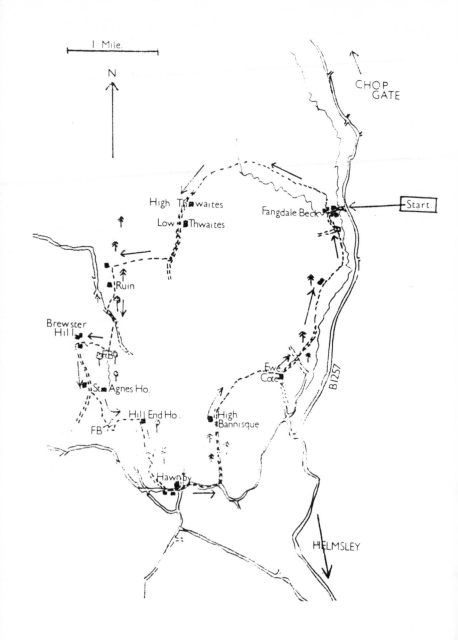

1 Mile.

N

CHOP GATE

High Thwaites
Low Thwaites
Fangdale Beck
Start.

Ruin

Brewster Hill

Ewe Cote

St. Agnes Ho.

B1257

Hill End Ho.
High Bannisque

FB

Hawnby

HELMSLEY

18

track which curves leftwards round the wall and passes to the right of the farm.

Continue south to Low Thwaites. The excellent views of the Hambleton hills now open up before you. The most easterly is Easterside, with Hawnby Hill on its right.

Walk on until a line of grouse butts crosses the path at right-angles (GR 546936). Turn right here and follow the path beside the butts through short heather in a westerly direction. The path crosses Hawnby Moor to the corner of a forest. Descent the sloping hillside on the right of the forest edge, towards a ruined building. Before reaching the building, look for a gate on your left, giving access to the forest (GR 531936).

Passing through the gate go along a green path with an old stone wall on the left. The path leads to a clearing, where boulders in the grass indicate a ruin. Keeping to the same direction cross this clearing and continue straight ahead on a wide grassy track between the trees, until it meets another green forest path at a T-junction. Here turn right and, ignoring all forks and crossroads, head SSW to a stone wall beside a tarmac road. The road is reached via a metal stile beside a gate a few yards to the right (GR 530929).

Turn left along the road for a short distance and when it curves to the right, look for a stile on the right and cross it. There is another stile immediately ahead but disregard this and turn left to walk downhill with the wall on your right, descending gradually through the wood on a sometimes sunken path.

The path drops abruptly to a T-junction with a wide forest path running N–S. Head left and south on the path as it curves gently right, left and right again, until a gap in the trees on the right gives the view of a green path. This is, again, sunken in places, and littered with small tree stumps in the long grass to trip the unwary. Follow the path gradually downhill through the forest to the river Rye and a footbridge which you should cross (GR 529922).

The path to the right along the riverbank is faint but soon leads to the ford where a clear track curves left to a gate. Pass through and go straight ahead across dry pastureland and towards a ruin. Keep this to the right as you continue west through another gate, then turn immediately left up the hillside keeping right of the fence. Cross a broken down stone wall and follow a clear forest path to the left, heading SSW.

Half a mile of easy and pleasant walking, with views of Rydale opening up on your left, brings you to Harker Gates, an elevated house and garden on the left. Immediately past the house, seek a small wooden stile on the left. Descend the hill to the left of boggy ground to join and follow the farmtrack from St. Agnes House in a southerly direction.

The dry clear path eventually crosses a small plank footbridge (GR 531907). Take the second of the two gates on the left, heading downhill and west, to cross a small footbridge. Then turn left and follow the path running through woodland and curving right and climbing fairly steeply, to a point where a gate to the left leads to open pasture.

Turn your back on this gate, and follow the path heading south through the woods to emerge shortly into a meadow. Continue south, passing below and to the right of Carr House. Head for a small stile in the bottom right hand corner of the meadow. The farm track from Carr House should be joined on the left, and followed southeast to the metalled road in Hawnby.

At the road, turn left past the Hawnby Hotel. Alternatively, call in at the hotel for refreshments. Walkers may call, leaving muddy boots at the door if necessary, to sample the daily bar lunch.

Continue east to the crossroads then follow the signpost to Laskill. Climb the steep twisting road, ignoring all other footpaths, until you see a sign on the left to "High Banniscue—Bed & Breakfast". Turn left along the well-defined track between conifer plantations. Those to the left are not shown on the map.

At High Banniscue Farm, follow the marked route round the right side of the farm building, and head north through the last farm gate onto open pasture. Continue to keep the fence on the right and cross two fields in a NE direction, to a solid wall. The route is unclear at this point but the map indicates a footpath crossing the corner to the right, and thence to a gate. Access is easy enough and after negotiating the gate in the wall to your right, go straight ahead on a faint but fast widening path running NE, round Pepper Hill and across the short heather.

The path eventually descends, curves east and heads towards a gate leading into an enclosed farm track to Low Ewe Cote Farm, where the track is clearly waymarked between the farm buildings. From the farm, walk NE on the farm track to reach a tarmac road. This is signposted "Wethercote Farm" to the left. Cross the road and go through the gate straight ahead. Continue on a clear track enclosed in places, which enters a wood in a NE direction and leads downhill through another gate into pasture.

Keep the fence/wall on the right, pass through two fields then go through a gate and turn right. Walk along the side of the next field. Turn left at the corner, and pass through a gate in the fence on your right. With the fence now on the left, head north again. Go through another gate and continue on the farm track to pass Helm House on the left, cross a tarmac road, and walk straight on in a NNE direction with the wall on your left for two fields. Turn right at the far corner of the second and head east towards the river Seph.

On the sometimes enclosed, and occasionally muddy track, continue NNW towards Malkin Bower where the tarmac road bears left to Fangdale Beck. Turn right in the village, and walk past cottages and the post office on your left to the T-junction, then down the road towards your car and the footbridge.

4. Chopgate–Tripsdale–Bransdale–Botton Head–Hasty Bank–Cold Moor Circular

Distance: 15 miles.
Start: Chopgate car park on the B1257 (GR 559994).
Maps: NYM Leisure Map. West Sheet.
  NYM Tourist Map.
Conditions: Moorland tracks and dales with plenty of climbing. Total ascents about 2,500 feet.

FROM the car park, turn right along the B1257, passing Esp House on the left. Turn left into the next farm access road to William Beck Farm. There are two gates to negotiate before swinging right immediately in front of the farm house. Follow the path beside the house wall then bear right on a grassy track; go through a gate and continue uphill on a sunken path between stone walls. Now go straight forward, still climbing, and through two more gates to reach open moorland.

Continue uphill and pass through a gap in a stone wall. Shortly, turn right on a clear track, then left where a broader, bulldozed, track crosses. This path eventually narrows and then descends, zig-zagging through heather and bracken to the lovely and uninhabited valley of Tripsdale. Just above the tree line, bear right and down to the beck which is easy to ford unless in flood.

At the other side, go diagonally left uphill and follow another zig-zag path to the moor top. Here a broader track continues eastwards, later swinging right and across Slapworth Moor with the shallow depression of Tarn Hole on the right. Keep on until another track feeds in from the left, a total distance of about 1½ miles from Tripsdale Beck. A few yards further on you will pass Stump Cross on the right of the path. Immediately, angle left across the heather, following a narrow path along a line of cairns and heading SE.

Descend in the same direction into Bransdale, with improving views of this green valley and of the long ridge of Rudland Rigg beyond it. Continue in a SE direction through heather and bracken then on a sunken track to join a minor tarmac road beside a footpath sign.

(If you wish to cross the valley through the fields and climb the Rigg directly, go straight across this road to follow public rights-of-way shown on your map. When you reach the top of the Rigg turn left to join the route described below.)

The main walk now passes through the pleasant mature woods

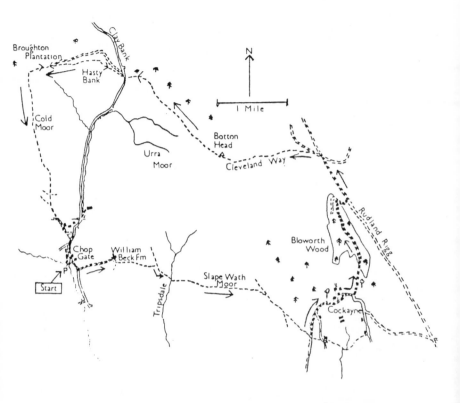

around the small community and church at Cockayne. Turn left on the road and walk towards the head of Bransdale, passing through a gate. Go over a bridge, crossing Hodge Beck, and a cattle grid. Bear right at the crossroads and after another cattle grid and bridge, walk uphill until the road turns sharp right.

Turn left at this point through a gate. The next mile and a half is not a right-of-way but is a permitted path. Go straight across the field and through another gate to join a Forestry Commission Track. This rises gently through woodland ensuring a pleasant ascent to Rudland Rigg.

After approximately one mile, on emerging from the trees, turn sharply right uphill through a gate. Keep on, joining and turning left on the broad track along the Rigg to reach Bloworth Crossing, half a mile further on. At this crossing a railway line used to carry iron ore across the moors between Rosedale and Middlesbrough. At the crossing of tracks, turn left on the old railway track, heading west.

23

Keep straight on until approximately 50 yards before the track curves right, leave it on a track to the left. Marked only by a post at the time of writing, this is the Cleveland Way which you follow for the next few miles. Continue in a north westerly direction over heather covered moor, passing a triangulation point on Round Hill marking the highest place on the North Yorkshire Moors at 1490 feet or 454 metres.

Continue on a clear path for further mile and a half, gradually descending to a gate. The descent then steepens and passes through a rocky defile before dropping to the B1257, Stokesley to Helmsley road.

The road is almost always busy so care should be taken when crossing. Go straight across and immediately climb, first on steps then on a track beside a wall. When the wall ends there is a choice of routes.

To follow the scenic route of the Cleveland Way, cross a large stile on the left and continue towards the steep climb up and over Hasty Bank. On descending the path goes through the shattered rock faces and clefts of The Wainstones, well frequented by rock climbers. Then continue forward across a grassy field keeping a wall on the left, and heading for the next hill, Cold Moor.

(For those tired of climbing, an alternative, lower route can be followed by continuing on the wide, permitted Forestry track, curving around and below Hasty Bank through the trees. On the plain below right are the villages of Great Broughton and further away, Great Ayton and Stokesley. Roseberry Topping and Captain Cook's Monument can also be seen through the occasional breaks in the trees. When the trees end on the left and you can look back at the Wainstones, go left over a stile in the fence and forward diagonally across the field passing a large boulder. Continue with a stone wall on your left towards Cold Moor.)

At this point the two routes join up again. Go through a gate at the foot of Cold Moor, and climb to the highest point at 1,317 feet or 402 metres. Once on the top, turn left away from the escarpment and head south along the ridge of the moor.

Bilsdale is on the left as you continue on a clear path through heather, towards the distant mast of the Bilsdale Transmitter. Soon after you begin to descend, about a mile from leaving the edge of the escarpment, the path forks. Bear left and descend, gently at first then quite steeply, towards Bilsdale.

From a rough defile the path contiues more faintly on grass. Now keep level, and parallel with the valley, as you continue towards the mast of Bilsdale Transmitter. Pass to the right of a group of trees, then walk beside the wall and downhill to pass through a gate.

On a sunken, and usually muddy, enclosed track, descend to the tarmac road, beside the Wesleyan chapel. Go forward between the houses to the main road. Turn right to walk on the pavement past the Buck Inn and the remaining yards back to the car park.

5. Blakey Ridge-Farndale-Sleightholme Dale-Shaw Ridge

Distance: 11 or 17 miles.
Starting point: Car park on Blakey Ridge, just past the Lion Inn (GR 684989).
Alternative shorter walk of 11 miles starting from Low Mill (GR 673953).
Maps: NYM Leisure Map. West Sheet.
*   Landranger 94.*

Conditions: Moors and meadows. Quite strenuous with three moderate ascents; total ascents above 2,300 feet.

WALK south on the road to Hutton-le-Hole for approximately half a mile. There is an embankment about 50 yards away from the road on the right. This is a dismantled railway track. When it ends, turn off the road to the right and, clipping the corner of this embankment, turn left to follow a path through heather. It heads diagonally downhill towards Farndale in a south westerly direction, faint at first but becoming clearer. Aim for a solitary tree beside the corner of a stone wall and go through the gate to walk downhill on a slightly sunken track.

Cross the next field diagonally, heading south and, going through a gap in the corner of the wall, walk on with the wall on your right. Pass through another gate, then turn along the farm track in a SW direction to a gate to join the tarmac road. Walk across the road and down a farm track, passing High Bragg House on the right.

On reaching the next set of buildings, Bragg Farm, keep these on the left and continue forward towards the River Dove. Turn left and walk for over a mile downstream on the famous daffodil walk, cross a footbridge and join the road at Low Mill. The shorter walk starts from here.

Turn left and walk along Mill Lane towards Gillamoor until it turns sharp left. At this point, leave the road, cross a stile and follow a path uphill in a westerly direction, passing a house on the left. Cross several stiles and keep to the left of the wall.

Good views of Farndale develop as the track climbs in a SE direction to disused quarries. The path now continues through heather and when it forks, turn left and head SE, making for the corner of a small plantation. Keep the plantation on the left and, on seeing a gate in the plantation wall, look for and take a path swinging right and SW through the heather.

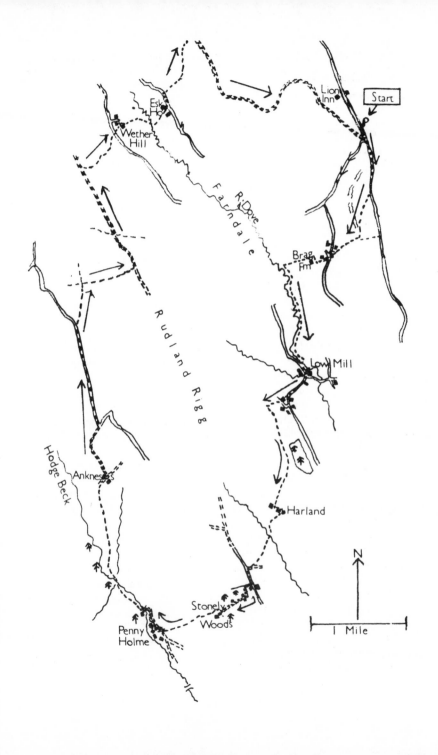

Start

Lion
Inn

Esk
Ho

Wether
Hill

R. Dove

Farndale

Brag
Fm

Rudland Rigg

Low Mill

Hodge Beck

Ankness

Harland

Stonely
Woods

Penny
Holme

N

1 Mile

Pass a prominent, pointed stone at the highest point on the moor and note the developing views of Sleightholme Dale. Descend towards the corner of a wall and walk beside and to the right then the left of it towards Harland Farm, passing through two gates.

Turn left on the farm track for the length of the field then turn right through a farmyard, and go forward through a gate. Follow the track over a green field, heading SW, to a gap in the fence and continue descending with a fence on the right, to a wall running parallel to Harland Beck (GR 667925).

Veer left and SE, and continue until reaching a recessed gate in the wall on the right. Go through this and cross the beck. Follow the path uphill through a gap in a wall, and cross the field diagonally to a gate leading into a planted area. A faint, and sometimes wet, path heads south-west through the trees to a gate and a tarmac road.

Turn left and walk along the road for approximately 400 yards, then turn right along the Hope Inn farm track. Shortly, turn left and then right, to pass Common House. (Note that School Plantation marked on the OS maps was being cut down in 1986, and will, presumably, be replanted.)

Continue on the path, which passes through what remains of the trees and goes past a small house on the left. At the Stonely Woods sign, take a track through the woods to the right, pass through a gate into an open meadow and turn left.

Keeping the woods and fence on the left, walk south west along the edge of the field. When the woods curve leftwards, leave the corner and head in the opposite direction (W), following a line of trees downhill to the corner of a wall. Walk on the right of this wall, then go through a gate and over a stile.

Head downhill through the heather in a westerly direction, descending steeply towards the corner of the field where the fence meets the wall. Go through a gate onto the tarmac lane. Turn right along the lane, passing Pennyholme on the left. Follow the track over a ford at Hodge Beck and past Otterhills, walking on with woods on the left until the track enters a wood.

Here, take a path to the right which curves as it descends to a new ford, and cross Hodge Beck once more at Mitchell Hag Wath (GR 640919). Immediately after the beck, turn left and cross a second stream on stepping stones. Follow a faint path up Ankness Ridge, keeping in a NNW direction through deciduous trees, winding between bracken and heather and arriving eventually at a gate in the corner of a stone wall.

With the wall on the right walk across a meadow and join a farm track, turning right on a walled lane to Ankness. Keep the farm buildings on the left and curve leftwards round them before turning right to walk through meadows, finally passing through a gate to emerge on the Bransdale road.

Turn left and walk along the road for one mile before turning right on a double track through the heather, marked "No access for Vehicles". Follow this track until a track crosses it at right angles. At this point, turn right and east past grouse butts (GR 634967). Drop to a stream, then climb to the broad track on Rudland Rigg. (For those doing the shorter walk from Low Mill, cross this track and descend on a track in a south-east direction to return to your starting point.)

Continuing with the main walk, turn left along Rudland Rigg and after about a mile, turn right along a grassy track (GR 635986), dropping to Farndale in a north easterly direction. The path descends gently at first and then steeply, to a stone enclosure. Go through this, and follow a clear green path downhill, turning left at another stone wall to a gate near a telegraph pole. Through the gate, descend to a tarmac road.

Cross the road and follow the footpath sign to Wether Hill Farm, passing between the farm buildings and slightly right through a gate into a long field. Follow the path gently downhill, then through two fields, veering right across a third field, and heading for a stone stile in the wall near the beck. Cross the beck and walk uphill, keeping the fence on the right. Cross a stile and turn left and go through the farm buildings of Esk House, onto a tarmac road.

Turn left on the road, and shortly afterwards, turn right along a public bridleway which climbs uphill, with a wall on the right. When the wall ends, follow the lower track heading north east and passing several stone walls as it climbs the hill towards the disused Farndale railway track.

Keep the brick building on the horizon to your right as you ascend, now heading north until you reach the railway path by a sign indicating the Esk Valley walk. Turn right and follow the track as it curves round High Blakey Moor for three miles back to the starting point.

6. Kildale-Roseberry Topping-Commondale-Baysdale Circular

Distance: 19 miles.
Start: Kildale (GR 605095) railway station or on main street near telephone box. There are several other possible starting points, for example Commondale (GR 656105) on open ground beside the road, or Gribdale Gate car park (GR 592110).
Maps: NYM Leisure Map. West Sheet.
*   Landranger 93 and 94.*
Conditions: Moor, forest and valley. Some mud in bad weather. Allow plenty of time for this long walk. No major ascents, about 1,900 feet overall.

BEGIN at the triangular roundabout opposite Kildale Hall Farm on the main road of the village. Walk briefly towards the railway station before turning right on a minor road signposted "Cleveland Way". This well-defined footpath will be followed for the next six and a half miles to Guisborough Woods.

Gradually bear right and uphill to Bankside Farm. Go through a gate and on the farm track, past the farm, gaining more height as you walk between the trees of Pale End Plantation.

At the top, turn left on a forest path but soon turn off following the signposted Cleveland Way footpath. Continue on this through woodland, ignoring all deviations, until you pass through a gap in a wall close to the 60 feet high Captain Cook's Monument. The obelisk, built in 1827, is sited at one of the finest viewpoints on the northern escarpment.

Turn right from the monument on a wide path bearing slightly rightwards of the distant Roseberry Topping. Then on a forest track, keep right and downhill to pass through a gate to the road at Gribdale Gate. Cross the road and, following the direction indicated by the Cleveland Way sign, go steeply uphill on a maintained path then keep on a grassy path to the right of a wall for about a mile. At a signpost beside the next gate, turn diagonally right to follow the Cleveland Way east across the moor to another gate beside a wood on the left.

Through the gate, turn right on a path around the wood to a junction of paths. Here turn right through another gate onto the moor. Go forward, bearing left (E then NE) and heading for the corner of wall boundaries around the fields of Highcliff Farm on the left.

30

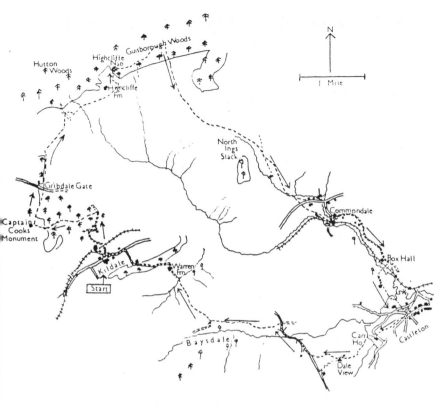

Keep beside the wall until it ends, then go through a gate on the left. Walk briefly beside a wall, then bear away right through the trees. Cross a forest path diagonally and climb gradually through woodland. The path levels and continues on to Highcliffe Nab. Just before the escarpment, turn right to climb steeply to the top of the Nab to enjoy the extensive view. Follow the path to a broad forest track and turn left along it.

Continue for nearly one mile before taking the second clear exit on the right, where you should see, and quickly reach, the open moor via a gate. Go forward across the heather moor in a southerly direction, passing two cairns. Keep to the higher ground above forest on the left but below the summit of Penrod Hill on the right, as the path swings left in a south easterly direction.

When the path begins to descend, stay left of North Ings Slack and the infant Whiteley Beck. Pass an old rail goods waggon, cross a track, then continue on a path through heather which gradually

31

drops to the beck before rising, briefly on a pannier track, to the Commondale-Kildale road.

Cross the road, and where the walls converge in a V opposite a small fenced copse, go through a gate. Keep beside the wall on your right, as you cross the fields through another two gates. Continue downhill on a rough lane passing the large brick built Lodge House. Turn left at the tarmac road, zig-zag uphill then turn right towards Commondale railway station.

Do not descend to the station, but go forward passing a bungalow on the left then bearing left then right on a walled track. Keeping above and left of the railway, continue on this clear track for just over one mile to the buildings of Box Hall. Before you in silhouette on the distant hillside is the village of Castleton.

Walk past Box Hall, then at the end of the first field on the right, leave the track and drop right to a gate. Go straight down the side of the field and cross the railway by two gates. Continue forward to cross Commondale Beck by a wooden footbridge, then go forward uphill until a clear track crosses before a wall. Go left around an earth mound, and right through a gate between the wall and a fence. Walk in a southerly direction and join the farm track to Scale Foot.

Go through the farmyard between the buildings, then continue forward downhill beside the hedge to the corner of the field. Bear left through a gap then cross the footbridge over the River Esk. Now walk diagonally left to the field end, then right uphill to cross a stile beside a tree. Continue forward and through a wicket gate. From here cross the first of two metalled roads, walking straight ahead over rough grass keeping to the left of a road sign on the horizon which marks the second road.

Refreshments can be obtained by making a short detour to the left, into Castleton village. Otherwise, go straight across the road and onto the rough grassland in front of you. This is shown on the map as Rigg End (GR 681078), the reference being the end of Castleton Rigg, which lies to the south. Bear right in a SW direction across the moor, shortly going gradually downhill and past a boundary stone. This stone is the third of three, counting from the first on the road.

Continue forward through rough moorland until, over the brow of a ridge, views of Westerdale reveal themselves. Before a wall go right on a grassy track which soon swings left to descend, gently at first then steeply, beside the wall to a road. There are steps set in the final few feet to the road, which continue at the far side of the road, beside the buildings of Carr House.

Bear to the right of the farm on a green path then go left through a gate onto the farm track. Go across the field, then right over a stream on a wooden footbridge. Walk uphill and through a metal gate, ignoring the first and lower gate. Continue with a wall on the right across the field to pass through the leftmost of two gates. Now with the River Esk on the left, walk along the top of two fields then in the next, swing right and uphill with the wall on your right.

At a wooden gate in the top left corner of the field, continue on a farm track with a wall on the left, which swings left to the buildings of Dale View. Pass to the right of the farm, and head towards a gap in the first field wall on the right, leading to the open moorland of Westerdale Moor. Continue NW, climbing gently across the moor and turn left at a signpost in a westerly direction. At the end of a line of grouse butts, bear left on a footpath to the tarmac road.

Turn right and walk along the road as it descends to cross the ford at Hob Hole, then climbs steeply to the junction with the Castleton road. At the junction, turn off left on a signed bridleway, to walk about one and a quarter miles along Baysdale. On reaching the first of a group of ruins, turn and climb the hill on your right to cross Kildale Moor on a clear path through heather.

A sizeable cairn and a marker post are at the top. After passing through a gate, go slightly right and descend in a NNW direction, this being further defined by a tall chimney in Leven Vale below. Go through a marked gate, and walk down the left edge of the field,

then join an unmetalled track. Follow this through two gates then passing the chimney and disused workings, go uphill to Warren Farm, seen on the skyline.

Go through the gate beside the farm, then continue eastwards on the track which at this point is marked as concessionary only. Although this unmaintained road does not entirely coincide with the right of way, the landowner has given consent for the concessionary path to be used by walkers.

Now descend through Kildale wood to the main road then turn left to walk on the footpath opposite, towards Kildale. You will soon reach the triangular roundabout in Kildale, and your starting point.

7. Lealholm-Fairy Cross-Fryup-Glaisdale Rigg.

Distance: 13½ miles.
Start: Car park in Lealholm village (GR 763077).
Maps: NYM Leisure Map, East Sheet.
*   Landranger 94.*
Conditions: Fields, pasture and moorland. Careful map-reading is
necessary in the first few miles through farmland but the clear hillside
and moorland tracks that follow are well worth the initial trouble.
Total ascents about 1,600 feet, with two climbs of 500 and 600 feet.

ON leaving the car park turn right on the tarmac road and walk uphill past the churches. Cross the railway bridge and turn left towards the station buildings on a rough road. Pass behind the railway buildings and before the road ends turn right through a gate and climb gently on a wide grassy track.

At a concourse of paths and gates, where the wall on the right swings right, follow it briefly downhill. Turn off left on a gently rising track and follow it, swinging right and up to a gate. Go through the gate, then bear right along the edge of two fields in a NNE direction. These are separated by a stone stile which is, unusually, built in a hedge.

At the end of the second field, turn right through a gate marked with a "Beware of the Bull" sign and bear left in the pasture, keeping a wary eye on the bull if present. A few yards take you to safety across the first of two stone stiles. Keep to the highest point as you proceed to cross two fields then follow the jagged edge of woodland to the far corner of the third.

Turn left through an opening into a rough field where the path appears to have been diverted. You should turn right and go forward along the right edge of this field and through a gate set in a wire fence into the main field. Go forward across the pasture and leftwards towards the woods, then walk beside the woods to the corner of the field.

Cross the stile beside the first of two gates, cross a stream and go through the second gate. Then angle right and climb uphill, heading west. Go through a gate set between a wall and a hedge and continue across the next field, still bearing west. Keeping to the left of a wall, head on a clear grassy path, then a farm track, towards the ruined buildings of Hole-i'-th'-Ellers.

The route bears right around the houses and through an iron gate. Now go diagonally left across the field, following the line of cabled posts to cross a stone stile in the wall. Descend briefly, ignoring a gate on the right, to swing right and continue with a stone wall on your right through two fields.

On approaching the buildings of Lawns Farm, continue on a walled green track and through a gate to the farmyard. Before the buildings turn right towards the wooden barn and climb, firstly on the maintained steps, then on a walled track which soon descends again. Continue forward through two gates with a wall on the left. Walk diagonally downhill across the field and into the next, and pass a gate at the road side to climb the wooden stile. Go straight across the roads through another gate.

Continue forward on the left side of the field, and across the railway line by two gates then forward again across the open field, passing to the right of a telegraph pole. Cross the River Esk on a sleeper bridge, then continue straight ahead, along the edge of fields on a rough cart track to the tarmac road.

Turn right on the road and pass the walls of three fields on the left. Before the next wall, go left through a gate into a field and forward past another gate to the field corner. Follow the wall left and uphill on a rough track in an eastwards direction. Where the path forks, keep on the right of way by bearing left on a green path which descends beside a wall to a stone stile, presently hidden behind gorse bushes. On the tarmac road, go right, then almost immediately right again, on the farm track to Head House.

The steep climb leads to the farm buildings but just before these your path swings right around them and continues beside a wall to a gate, and beyond it close to the walled right edge of fields.

There are excellent views of Eskdale below to the right. When you go through a gate where the wall ends, swing away from the escarpment and on the right of way, climb diagonally across the heather and bracken moorland going south.

After approximately one third of a mile swing rightwards and south-west towards a wooded hill on the horizon. The path descends again to the escarpment edge under the aforementioned wooded hill, and above walled fields. Little Fryup Dale lies below to the right.

Where the path forks under the pine trees near a large rock, go forward on the upper and left path towards another stand of pines. Continue beside the wall, then turn right to descend to go through a gate onto a walled green track. Go down to the T-junction, then turn left and walk on to another gate, leading to the road.

Turn left along the road past the buildings at Fairy Cross, and at the road junction turn right to follow the sign to Fryup Head. Where

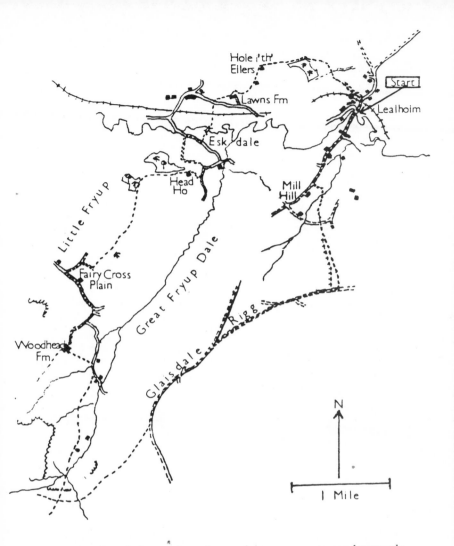

the road swings left, continue forward on a concrete road towards Woodhead Farm. After passing the farm buildings, the walled track forks. Go left and downhill through a gate, then cross a field to a stile beside a tree to reach the road.

Now turn briefly right, and then, when the road turns left, go right through a gate marked with a footpath sign to Rosedale. Angle rightwards through a gap in the wall. On reaching three gates, go through the middle one, and continue climbing beside a hedge. After the next field and gate continue along on a green path beside

37

fences and walls. Keep on climbing steadily on the right side of the dale towards Great Fryup Head.

The path passes to the right of an old sheepfold and continues, skirting below old spoilheaps. When the fence ends, go forward across rough moorland and through a gate below an iron hut. Angle left down to cross the stream, then zig-zag right and steeply uphill in a southwards direction. Small but picturesque waterfalls are numerous on the rock faces around the head of this dale, which must

be a good contender for the most impressive valley head on the North York Moors.

When the slope flattens out at the top, go straight on to a cairn where you turn left on a broad track, curving around the eastern edge of the dale. This wide track leads clearly in a north-easterly direction through heather and bilberries for one mile before reaching the metalled road at a bridleway sign.

Go left along the road for approximately one mile, until, where the road swings left continue forward on a broad rough track marked "Unsuitable for vehicles". It enables easy walking along the summit of Glaisdale Rigg.

After 1½ miles (GR 760049), a green track crosses the main route. Turn left on it towards the prominent row of boundary stones, then continue on this track beside the stones in a northerly direction until they end. Then keep forward across the rough moor, gradually descending in the north north-west direction set by the last two boundary stones. Swing slightly left to cross the end of a line of well hidden grouse butts, and continue down to the tarmac road.

Cross the road and, in the direction indicated by a "Bridleway" sign, cross a rough field to a "V" formed between fence and wall. Go through the gate, then down the right hand edge of the field and through two gates on opposite sides of a ditch. Keep right as you walk on, then finally descend leftwards to cross Busco Beck on a footbridge. Go through the next gate and briefly forward in the field, then swing left and cross the field in a north west direction, keeping right of the buildings at Mill Hill. On the far side, go through a gate found at the end of the wall running from the house.

Once on the tarmac road bear right and downhill to Lealholm village and the car park.

8. Wheeldale Gill-Hamer Moor-Muffles Rigg-Raindale-Simon How Circular.

Distance: 19 miles.
Start: Wheeldale road. Room for several cars on grass on the north side of the ford at Wheeldale Gill. (GR 801992).
Maps: NYM Leisure Map. East Sheet.
Landranger 94.
Conditions: Mainly moorland and forest. Fairly flat walking, total ascents about 1,200 feet.

CROSS the ford going south, and continue on the road climbing fairly steeply. At the brow of the hill turn right onto a clear track, soon branching right where signposted on the Lyke Wake Walk. Follow the clear broad track over the moor, after two and a half miles from the start passing the large standing stone at Blue Man i' th' Moss, eventually to join a minor moorland road (GR 744995).

Turn left and walk on the road briefly, leaving it to the left on a signed footpath. Head towards a barn, and then to the right of the walls around it. Just beyond the last wall, where the paths divide, the clearer path descends gently to the right, but continue straight ahead in a south east direction through heather.

On reaching a fence, climb a stile by the gate, then over a small grassy hill. Descend towards Cropton Forest, aiming straight ahead for the lowest point where there is a gap in the trees. Keeping a small stream on your left, enter the forest by a stile beside a gate. The track is sometimes wet and overgrown in places but still clear, and marked by wooden posts.

Continue south, with trees of various sizes on the left and a stone wall or fence on the right, for just over a mile. At a junction, go forward on a clear farm track, through three gates, and passing St. James Farm.

Follow a clear forest track south for just over half a mile, ignoring waymarked signs. Just before the track turns sharply left, a footpath marked with yellow arrows crosses it (GR 765935). Turn left and eastwards on this grassy path between the trees. On joining a metalled road, follow it to the buildings of High Muffles. Here, at a junction of tracks, continue forward and east on the middle track.

At a T-junction, turn right on an unmetalled road, then at the next junction (GR 989935), continue forward to walk on a pleasant, fenced track which passes Stape Farm.

On reaching the tarmac road turn right for approximately one

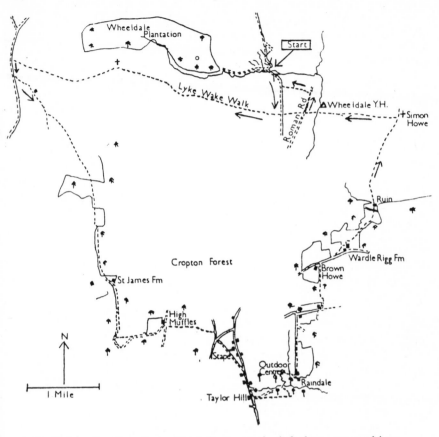

third of a mile. Pass Seavy Slack Farm on the left then, on reaching Taylor Hill, another farm on the right, turn left on an unmetalled road. Just before the road turns sharply left, pass through a gate on the right and walk on a grassy path along the left sides of fields, going east. There are views of Raindale to the left, and of Levisham Brow before you.

When a well-trodden fenced path crosses, turn left and downhill to Raindale. Cross Raindale Beck on a small footbridge, then bear left on a path which climbs steeply through the woods. At the top, cross a stile and turn left beside the fence to go right over another stile, and pass behind the Outdoor Centre. This path has been re-routed. Cross the courtyard, and follow a signposted path, eastwards, through bracken before descending steeply through woodland to cross a footbridge.

41

Go uphill to a shed, and cross a stile beside it. Turn right and cross the field leftwards, to join a clear unmetalled track. Turn left at this point and follow the track through a gate and past a barn. Walk north on the unmetalled road for two thirds of a mile then, at a T-junction, turn right to continue on the road going between High Raindale Head Cottage and Heads House.

At the Forestry Commission sign (GR 812941), turn left (N) on a grassy path with the forest on the right. The path keeps right of Brown Howe Farm and leads to a tarmac road. Turn right on the road, to walk past a small plantation, and Wardle Rigg Farm on the left. At the next plantation on the left, take a grassy path to the left, which leads to a forest road at right angles.

Go forward over a stile into open pasture (NE). Cross the field diagonally right towards the end of the plantation. Your way now lies over the fence to the right, then beside the forest. As there is, at present, no stile in the fence you may find it easier to walk a few yards further to a gate, then regain the path running beside the fence and trees on your right.

When this fence turns away sharply right, continue downhill to cross a track, then over a stile and down to the corner of the plantation, keeping it on the right. Keep close to the fence beside the trees, and walk downhill to a gate on the right of the ruined building of Wardle Green. Descend to a footbridge into open moorland, then head uphill towards the left of a stone enclosure on the skyline.

After passing the enclosure, bear across to your right heading NNE towards the higher ground on your right. Straight ahead, on the horizon, you should be able to see the two tumili of Two Howes. Wheeldale Beck runs away from you on the left.

The path through the heather climbs almost imperceptibly, and eventually the cairn of Simon Howe comes into view ahead. Continue to bear slightly to the left of this, until you pick up the broad track of the Lyke Wake Walk at Simon Howe itself. Turn left and west, and descend to Wheeldale. This valley, with its green meadows, is a strong contrast to the moorland behind.

Keep to the left of Wheeldale Lodge Youth Hostel, with the wall on your right. Go over a stile, then cross the beck on stepping stones. For those still with energy, continue upwards and forward on the Lyke Wake path.

For a more leisurely but longer ascent, take the path to your left, and climb gradually to reach the Roman Road. This road, one of the finest examples in Britain, crosses the moors from Pickering to Grosmont. Turn right to walk beside an exposed section of the ancient roadway, passing through an iron gate in a stone wall, and continue along the road for a short distance.

Turn left just before the next stone wall. Contour around the grassy hill, and go through the lower of two gates in a stone wall. Turn right and follow the tarmac road downhill to your starting place.

9. Saltergate-Bridestone Griff-Newton Dale-Hole of Horcum.

Distance: 14 miles.
Start: Car park half-mile south of the Saltergate Inn on the A169.
(GR 853937).
Maps: NYM. Leisure Map, East Sheet.
      Landranger 100.
Conditions: Moderately strenuous walking through picturesque valleys, forests and moorland. Total ascents about 1,600 feet.

FROM the car park walk briefly rightwards on the road in a northerly direction, then turn off it to the right on a wide forest track. When the trees on your right end, turn left along the edge of the field, passing a gate on the left. Then bear right and continue in a NE direction on a field path along Saltergate Brow.

Where the path turns east and forks, take the right and higher, fork which soon descends, skirting the edge of the brow, to Malo Cross. Turn right to walk south beside the forest on a clear track. The public footpath marked on the OS maps as running slightly lower down beside the forest edge is invisible, and the way is blocked by barbed wire fences.

When the track you are following takes you through a metal gate, descend diagonally to the lower path beside the forest. Cross the stile beside a white metal gate, then bear left uphill to a stile at the farm of Newgate Foot.

Turn right between the farm buildings, then left through two gates, continuing on a clear track through two fields. Just past the second line of trees turn right and uphill to cross a stile. Continue to climb beside the fence then cross another stile. Go straight forward to a stone cross and the unmetalled road.

Bear left, going SSE. Just before the track enters woodland, turn off it to the right through a gate and continue south on a broad track beside the forest. Take the first clear path to your right, which leads through heather and bracken to the Bridestones. Pass between them before your path curves and descends through mixed woodland to a squeezer stile.

To the left is the Foresty Commission car park, but your route goes immediately right through another stile, and continues down the main valley of Staindale. Skirt below the now uninhabited Low Staindale Farm, once a Youth Hostel, then negotiating stiles follow the occasionally faint path through grassland. A clearer path

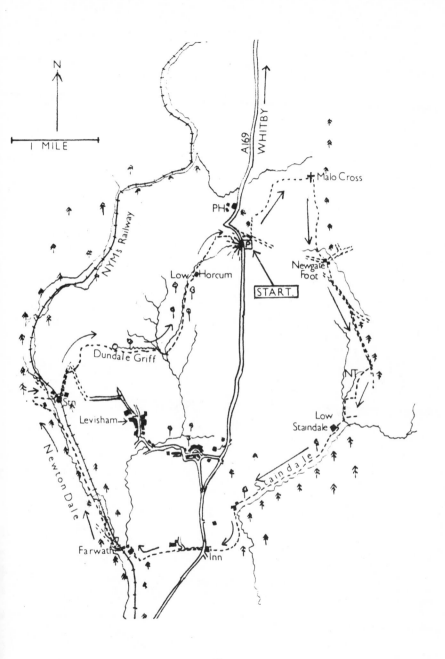

N

1 MILE

WHITBY

A169

NYMs Railway

Malo Cross

PH

P

START.

Low Horcum

Newgate Foot

Dundale Griff

NT

Stn

Levisham

Low Staindale

Newton Dale

Staindale

Farwath

Inn

continues in mature coniferous forest to a gate in front of the buildings of Staindale Lodge.

On the map the footpath is shown as bearing left and crossing the stream. However, the footbridge that enabled this to be followed with ease, is no longer there. Access is permitted through the next gate onto a private road. Almost immediately, turn left through a white gate in a stone wall and into open meadowland to head south.

Continue with the beck on your left past High Dalby House on a broad track. Halfway along the wall enclosing the grounds of High

Dalby House, climb directly uphill to cross a stile at the forest edge. Climb steeply on a forest path, to emerge in a field where the route lies rightwards keeping the woods to your left and bearing SW., then W.

When the trees and the field come to an end, go forward on a narrow, overgrown path, then along the left side of two more fields, passing a caravan site. Keep well to the right and following the signs, pass the Fox and Rabbit Farm and the inn of the same name, then cross the A169 road.

Go straight ahead on an unmetalled road which is metalled further on. When it curves right, continue forward (W) through a gate. Pass between hedges then across an open field to descend diagonally right to the valley floor, well left of Farfields Farm. Cross a stile beside a white gate to descend, steeply at first, down the valley of Crossdale.

At the bottom, turn right across a small stream and continue forward through two gates. Take a left turn to pass between the railway buildings at Farworth Crossing. In the summer months this station is one of the stopping points for the steam trains of the North York Moors Railway.

Once across the concrete bridge, go briefly right on a broad track, and turn off it to the right on another path known as Bottoms Road. This path continues parallel to the railway for two miles in a north westerly direction down the steep-sided Newton Dale. The path is mainly in woodland, but occasionally in open meadow and water meadows.

Near Levisham, the next station on the line, the track curves uphill passing through several gates and some rough and overgrown pasture. On coming to an open space, and before electricity lines cross overhead, turn right and zig-zag downhill to a broad path. Follow this to Levisham Station and cross the railway line.

Continue forward then left on the tarmac road, soon dropping down to a sunken, grassy path beside a wall. Climbing to the road, cut its corner and aim straight ahead for a path going diagonally left up the hillside before you.

At the top of the steep climb, go forward to the corner of a wall, then continue in a NE direction on open moorland, keeping the wall on your right. When it ends carry on, going east, towards Dundale Pond (GR 828919).

A number of paths meet at this point, but your route passes to the right of the pond and continues forward beside the tree-lined ravine of Dundale Griff. The track gently descends to a signpost. There, turn left, cross two small streams, then bear left and continue on a clear path beside a wall on the right. Carry on, in a NNE direction, towards the deep valley of The Hole of Horcum. Keep on a path between the forest and the beck which is below on the left. Bear left around the presently uninhabited Low Horcum Farm, then go forward to the point where the steep, well marked climb straight ahead begins. Here, swing right across the valley floor and through two gates into woodland. A steeply climbing path leads to the main A169 road, and returns you to the car park.

10. Jugger Howe Beck-Lownorth Beck-Blea Hill beck

Distance: 19 miles
Start: Plenty of room at the layby on the A171, half-mile south of the Flask Inn (GR 942004).
Maps: NYM Leisure Map. East Sheet.
     Landranger. Sheet 94.
Conditions: A beautiful but sometimes strenuous walk in varied conditions through valleys, meadows and moorland. The path along Jugger Howe Beck is very boggy in places and the beck floods badly in heavy rain. A compass is essential.

FROM your parking place at the NW end of the layby, look west for a wooden gate leading to fields. Climb the stile beside it and head SW, with a fence and the deepening valley of Burn Howe Dale on the left. Continue, climbing two stiles and at the end of the next field turn briefly right before passing through a gate. Keep on beside a hedgerow and fence, still going SW.

After approximately 100 yards, you reach a birch tree to the left of your path. Here, angle left and descend diagonally through bracken to a stream. Turn right beside the fence to cross a low

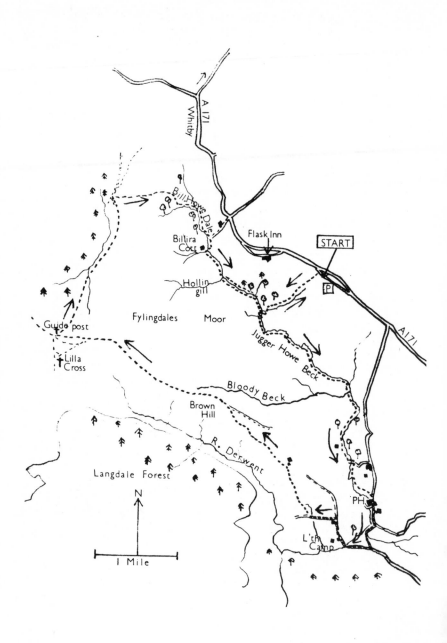

A171
Whitby

Bill Howe Dale

Flask Inn

START

P

Billira Cott

Holling ill

Fylingdales   Moor

Jugger Howe Beck

Guide post

Lilla Cross

A171

Bloody Beck

Brown Hill

R. Derwent

Langdale Forest

N

PH

L'th Camp

1 Mile

wooden footbridge. Once across, turn immediately left and follow a faint path on the right bank of Jugger Howe Beck. There follows a pleasant walk south along the valley cut by the beck, occasionally climbing higher on the right bank to avoid wet areas and overgrown scrub and deciduous trees.

Towards the end of the valley the route goes through attractive deciduous woodland. At a fork where the rightwards path turns uphill, bear left on a clearer cart track across a wooden bridge. Go uphill for a few yards, then through a gate on the right into a long meadow to walk south on the left bank of the stream.

Approximately 50 yards before the meadow ends, turn left on a diagonally climbing path through trees. In continues rightwards within the trees, then downhill once more beside a barbed wire fence to the first of two stiles. Once over these and across a minor stream, turn left to walk SSE on the edge of the field with a wood on the left.

Leave the field by the second opening on the left, then turn right and continue with woods on the right. Shortly, pass through two gates leading to the tarmac road by a cart track. Go right, pass the Mill Inn, then follow the Silpho and Hackness road. After about halfl a mile, turn right on the road to Low North Camp. Pass the camp on the left, and continue straight on in the direction of Langdale End.

Keep to the right of the buildings, then go left before the last barn on a sandy farm track. When you have passed two fences and a thin patch of trees on the right, take a clear broad field path on the right (GR 940958), leading uphill and through a wide gap between small conifer plantations. Go through two gates and walk across a rough field keeping a fence, and then a plantation on the right.

Then follow the edge of the wood left and downhill on a new farm track below River Head Farm, and turn right through a gate into the second field past the end of the plantation. Negotiate more gates as you cross a series of rough fields continuing NW towards the whaleback shape of Brown Hill. Pass to the right of Brown Hill and head towards a fence on the right. Follow the line of the fence to pass through a wicket gate on to a clear sandy moorland track.

Walk on for approximately one and a half miles to the Saltergate-Goathland Guide post. Just south of this post can be seen the prominent cross and cairn marking the tumulus of Lilla Howe. At the guide post, turn right off the main track and walk towards the sea, on a path running NE. Keep on this path, known as the Robin Hood's Bay Road, as it continues, gradually descending, to the right of the large Newton House Plantation.

Shortly after crossing the beck which issues from Leech Bog Slack, look to the left to see a small, but pretty, waterfall. From there the going is straightforward but sometimes indistinct through heather and across marshy ground as you head north for approximately one and a half miles. Blea Hill Beck runs between your path and the forest. Where the beck enters the forest, your route breaks away briefly uphill to the right, and is cairned for a short distance as it gradually swings away from the trees, through heather and bracken.

When the path descends to meet a clear broad track, follow this for a sort distance until arriving at the lowest point in a dip (GR 899018). Turn right off this track and walk east on the right bank of the shallow, marshy valley of Biller Howe Dale Slack. Continue until a stone wall is seen ahead, and near it, descend on a clearly cut track to the valley and cross the beck. Turn right and over a stile beside a gate into Ling Hill Plantation to begin a pleasant walk down Biller Howe Dale.

Continue south on a clear path through the wooded dale, keeping the stream on your right. Go through a gate into an open field and angle rightwards with the fence, and later a wall, on the right, going SE. When the wall ends, turn right through a gate and cross a small beck. Walk uphill on a clear track, then downhill and through another gate which at the time of writing was partially obstructed by a single strand of barbed wire.

Go forward briefly, then turn left across a wooden footbridge. Walk forward onto a farm road and turn right. Continue along the road and where it crosses the stream in front of Billira Cottage turn left along the right bank of the beck. Continue forward and cross a broken down wall.

Turn left and walk on with the wall and the beck on your left, occasionally climbing higher on the right to avoid wet ground. Where the path enters a small copse go through the wall and down towards the beck. From the minor dale of Hollin Gill, coming in from the right is a tributary stream which should be crossed near its junction with the main Brown Rigg Beck.

Your route now swings leftwards (WSW) as you continue down the main valley, again beside the wall, on a path which is sometimes boggy. On nearing a conifer plantation on the left go through the wall once more and cross the beck. On reaching the woodland, climb a stile beside a gate then continue beside the conifers, on the left bank of the beck. Cross the beck again, and continue until the deciduous woodland ends.

At this point, keep to the lower path and cross Jugger Howe Beck for the last time by a small sleeper footbridge (GR 930995).

From here, you retrace your route at the start of the walk. Turn briefly right beside a fence, then follow it left. After a few yards bear diagonally right uphill, then right upon reaching a hedge and fence. Follow the path in a NE direction, across the fields and back to your starting point.

Useful Addresses:

North York Moors National Park Offices, The Old Vicarage, Bondgate, Helmsley, York. Tel 0439 70657.
   Their wide range of services includes advice on public rights of way and passing on reported obstructions to Park Rangers.

North York Moors Railway, Commercial Manager, Pickering Railway Station, Pickering, YO18 8DA. Tel 0751 72508 or 73535.

Information and Visitor Centres at:
1. Danby Lodge National Park Centre, Lodge Lane, Danby, Whitby. Tel 02876 654.
2. Forest Visitor Centre, Low Dalby, Pickering. Tel 0751 60295.
3. National Trust Information Centre, Ravenscar. Tel 0723 870138.
4. Pickering Station Information Centre, North York Moors Railway, Pickering. Tel 0751 73791.
5. Sutton Bank Information Centre, Sutton, Thirsk. Tel 0845 597426.

Other Information

For details of annually organized (long) walks, contact: The Long Distance Walkers' Association. The Membership Secretary, 4, Mayfield Road, Tunbridge Wells, Kent. TN4 8ES.

The Rosedale Circuit. Route details from The Rosedale Circuit Secretary, British Aerospace Aircraft Group, Blackburn Welfare Society, Rambling Club Section, Brough, North Humberside. Send SAE.

Useful Publications

Lyke Wake Walk, Bill Cowley (Dalesman Books).
The Cleveland Way, Bill Cowley (Dalesman Books).
Cleveland Way Companion, Paul Hannon (Hillside Publications).
The Bilsdale Circuit, Michael Teanby (Dalesman Books).
The White Rose Walk, Geoffrey White (Dalesman Books).
Eskdale Way, Louis S. Dale (Dalesman Books).
The Crosses Walk, Malcolm Boyes (Dalesman Books).
The Forest Walk: Reasty to Allerston. Route details from the Walk Secretary, Forestry Commission, 42, Eastgate, Pickering. Send SAE.
Discover the North York Moors and Coast, Pat and Alan Staniforth (Discovery Guides).
Stone Causeways of The North York Moors, Bill Breakell (Footsteps Books).
Exploring the North York Moors, Malcolm Boyes (Dalesman Books).
A History of Rosedale, R.H. Hayes (North York Moors National Park).
Cameron's Guide to the Esk Valley Railway (Avon Anglia Publications).
Cleveland Ironstone Mining, John S. Owen (C Books).